THE BIG BOOK OF ART
DRAW! PAINT!
CREATE!

 Walter Foster Jr.

www.walterfoster.com
3 Wrigley, Suite A
Irvine, CA 92618

Illustrations on front and back cover and pages 1, 4, 5 (sketchbook, owl, spaceship), 12, 17, 22-24, 33, 38-40, 46, 47, 54-56, 60, 61, 71, 88, 89, 92, 93, 101, 120, 121, and 123 by Lisa Martin and Damien Barlow.

Artwork on back cover (ladybug) and pages 5 (hot air balloons and stained glass drawings), 7, 10 ("Acrylic Palette"), 18, 26-32, 48, 50-53, 58, 59, 62-70, 72-87, 90, 91, 94-100, 116-119, 125, and 127 by Elizabeth T. Gilbert.

Photographs on pages 6, 10 ("Watercolor Paint," "Watercolor Palette," "Acrylic Paint"), 11, 16, 102 ("Glue"), and 103 ("Paint," "Crayons") © Shutterstock.

Artwork on pages 34-37, 42-45, and 102-115 by Jennifer McCully.

Artwork on page 20 by Diana Fisher.

Publisher: Rebecca J. Razo
Creative Director: Shelley Baugh
Project Editor: Stephanie Meissner
Managing Editor: Karen Julian
Associate Editor: Jennifer Gaudet
Assistant Editor: Janessa Osle
Production Designers: Debbie Aiken, Amanda Tannen
Production Manager: Nicole Szawlowski
Production Coordinator: Lawrence Marquez

1 3 5 7 9 10 8 6 4 2

table of contents

getting started

Welcome to *The Big Book of Art: Draw! Paint! Create!*
Are you ready to learn how to make awesome art using all kinds
of fun art tools? In this book you'll explore making art with
crayons, colored pencils, markers, chalk, watercolors,
and acrylic paint. Then you'll learn how to combine all of
those to create fun mixed media art!

Look for the practice pages throughout the book to draw and color with crayons, colored pencils, or markers!

PRACTICE HERE

Use a sketchbook, drawing pad, or scrap paper to warm up and practice your art.

Tear out the four pages at the back of the book to help make your own masterpieces! You'll find a cute owl and an amazing space scene to color in with crayons, colored pencils, or markers. Use the hot air balloon drawing to help you get started with the project on pages 50-53. Use the stained glass drawing for the project on pages 58-59.

Ready to begin?
Turn the page to get started!

drawing tools

You can use all kinds of tools for drawing.

Pencil, Sharpener & Eraser

Crayons

Markers

Chalk

Colored Pencils

drawing basics

By starting with just a few basic shapes, you can draw almost anything!

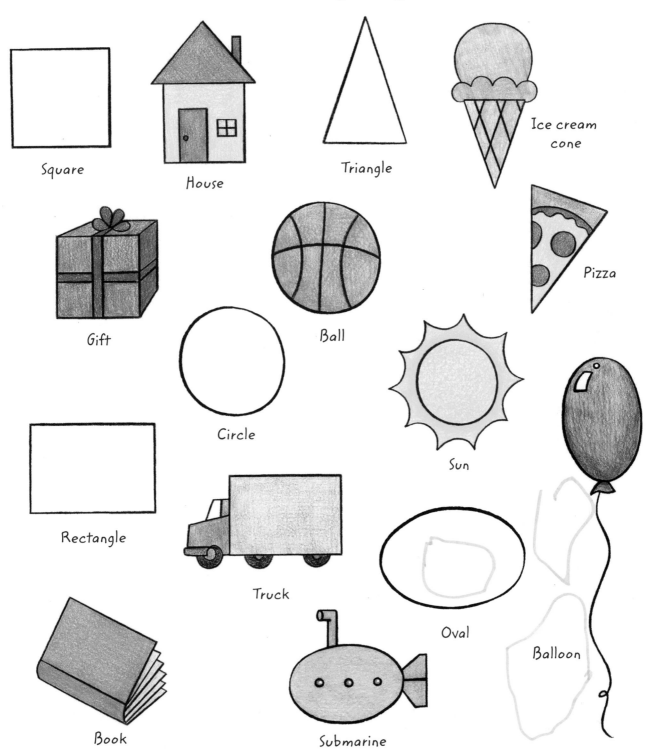

Square

House

Triangle

Ice cream cone

Gift

Ball

Pizza

Circle

Sun

Rectangle

Truck

Oval

Balloon

Book

Submarine

Practice drawing shapes, lines, and squiggles with your crayons, markers, and colored pencils. Below are some examples to get you started.

PRACTICE HERE

PRACTICE HERE

painting tools

Watercolor Paint Watercolor comes in tubes of moist paint or pots of dried paint. Just add water with a paintbrush.

Watercolor Palette A palette keeps tube paint colors separate and clean. You can also use small paper cups.

Acrylic Paint Acrylic paint is very thick, but you can thin it with water to make it look like watercolor.

Acrylic Palette You don't need a fancy palette for acrylic paint—try using a paper plate for your paints and a plastic spoon or your paintbrush to mix colors.

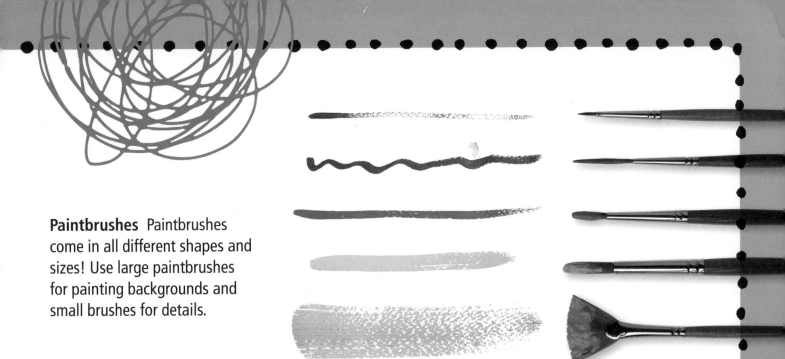

Paintbrushes Paintbrushes come in all different shapes and sizes! Use large paintbrushes for painting backgrounds and small brushes for details.

Paper Use thick watercolor paper when painting. You don't want the paint to bleed through! You can also paint on canvas with acrylic paint.

TIP Keep two cups of water nearby — one for rinsing your brushes and one for mixing clean water with your paint.

the color wheel

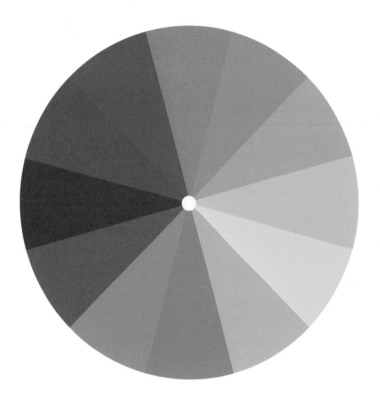

The color wheel shows us how colors relate to one another. Artists use the color wheel to understand the different colors and how to mix them.

There are three **primary** colors: red, yellow, and blue. These colors cannot be made by mixing other colors. But with these three colors, you can mix just about any other color you want!

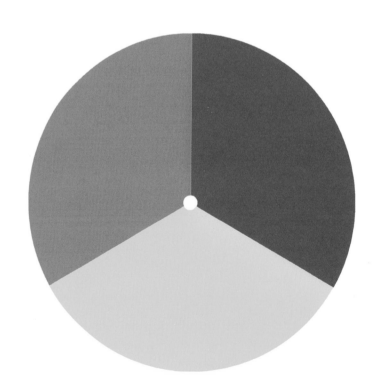

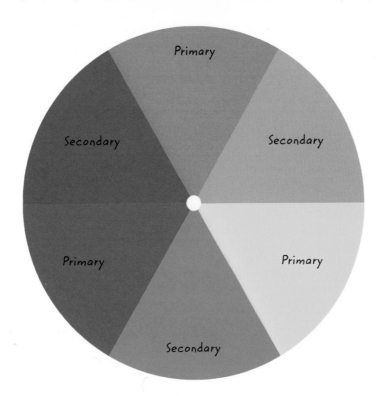

By mixing two primary colors, you can create a **secondary** color!
Orange, green, and purple are secondary colors.

Red + Yellow = Orange

Blue + Red = Purple

Yellow + Blue = Green

When you mix a primary color with a secondary color, you create a **tertiary** color. Tertiary colors are yellow-orange, red-orange, red-purple, blue-purple, blue-green, and yellow-green.

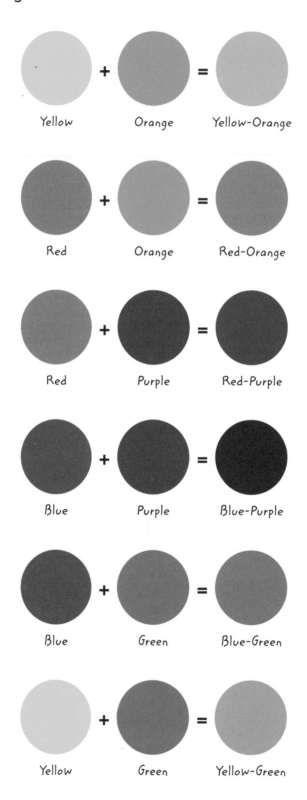

Yellow + Orange = Yellow-Orange

Red + Orange = Red-Orange

Red + Purple = Red-Purple

Blue + Purple = Blue-Purple

Blue + Green = Blue-Green

Yellow + Green = Yellow-Green

LIGHTENING WATERCOLOR PAINT

You can lighten watercolor paint by adding water. The more water you add, the lighter the color will become and the thinner the paint will be.

CREATING TINTS

You can lighten acrylic paint colors by adding white paint. The more white paint you add to the mix, the lighter the color will become.

Blue + White = Sky Blue

CREATING SHADES

You can darken any acrylic paint color by adding black paint. The more black you add, the darker the color will become.

Blue + Black = Navy

CREATING TONES

You can dull a color by mixing it with gray to create a softer, more muted version.

Blue + Gray = Slate

extra art materials

Below are a few extra art tools you will need as you work on the projects in this book.

Glue Stick

Scissors

Construction Paper

Ink Pad

Black Tempera Paint

TIP Tempera paint (also called "poster paint") is creamy and dries quickly. This is the best kind of paint for making scratchboard art!

getting creative

**Below are some ideas for using crayons.
Try some of them out on the opposite page!**

MIXING COLORS

Color over another color to make a new one. In this example, yellow on blue makes bright green.

CRISSCROSS

Draw straight lines next to each other. Then turn the paper and draw more straight lines over the first set.

COLORING DARK TO LIGHT

Press hard to create dark strokes. As you move down the paper, don't press as hard, making the color lighter as you go.

CRAYONS & WATERCOLOR

Wax crayons don't mix with water. Draw with white crayon, and then stroke over the drawing with watercolor paint. Your drawing will show through!

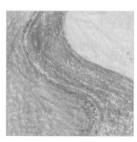 

MAKE A SCRATCHBOARD

Start by covering your paper with bright sections of crayon. Paint over the crayon with black tempera paint. Once dry, use a Popsicle stick to "draw" by scratching away the paint to reveal the colorful crayon underneath!

PRACTICE HERE

draw a UFO

PRACTICE HERE

crayon-imals

Try drawing these cute critters with crayons. It's fun and easy when you work step by step!

DRAWING IS FUN!

PRACTICE HERE

outer space scratch art

Create a glowing, out-of-this world space scene with just a few simple materials, including crayons, black tempera paint, and a Popsicle stick!

MATERIALS

* Thick paper
* Thin paper, such as printer paper
* Pencil
* Crayons in a range of bright colors

* Black tempera paint
* Large paintbrush
* Popsicle stick or other scraping tool
* Scissors

1 Trim a sheet of thick paper and a sheet of thin paper to the same size. Draw a space scene on the thin paper.

2 Use bright crayons to make bands of color on the thick paper. Press hard to cover all of the white space.

3

Use a large paintbrush to cover the paper with a thick layer of black tempera paint.

4

Once the paint is dry, the scratchboard is ready to use! Place the space scene drawing on top of the scratchboard. Trace it with a pencil to make an outline of the drawing on the scratchboard.

5

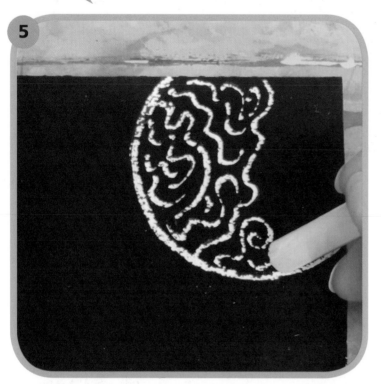

Use the edge of a Popsicle stick to scratch away the black paint to reveal the color underneath.

texture rubbings

Make fun and amazing art with crayon rubbings using coins, leaves, twigs, paper clips, or anything else you can find around your house and yard!

1

Place a leaf or other object between two sheets of paper.

Rub over the object with a crayon. The shape and texture of the object will show on the paper!

2

3

You can hold the crayon like a pencil or with the long side facing the paper (shown here).

4

Find leaves in all shapes and sizes. The thicker the leaf, the better!

Plenty of household items can create cool rubbings. Look around and see what you can find!

MESH COASTER

DOTTED NAPKIN

COIN

GLUE

Try using white glue to draw designs or letters on a sheet of paper. Once the glue dries, place a sheet of paper over it and create a rubbing!

markers

getting creative

You can create many different effects with markers. Use a combination of markers — thick, fine-tip, watercolor, or erasable — to make fun designs!

LOTS OF DOTS

Use lots of dots to draw. The more dots in an area, the darker that area will look. Use the very tip of a marker to create small, fine dots. Press harder to create larger dots.

CRISSCROSS

Fill a drawing with crisscrossed lines. The closer the lines are to each other, the darker an area will look. Use multiple colors to crisscross over each other and watch as new colors appear!

THICK & THIN

Marker tips make a difference! Use thick tips for coloring in large spaces and thin tips for writing and coloring in small spaces.

DRAWING WITH WATERCOLOR MARKERS

I drew the first scribbled yellow box on the right with a watercolor marker. I drew the second box with the same marker, and then I painted over it with a wet paintbrush. See how much softer this yellow box appears after adding water? While the paper was wet, I drew the blue star on top with another watercolor marker.

ADDING WATER

Adding water to different types of markers creates different effects. Some markers stay very bright, while others soften and fade.

Regular Markers + Water

Watercolor Markers + Water

making a print

"Monoprinting" is a fun way to transfer your artwork onto paper. No two prints look exactly the same. They are all different!

MATERIALS

* Thick paper
* Acrylic cutting board*
* Markers

* Spray bottle of water
* Construction paper (optional)
* Scissors (optional)

*Note: You can find acrylic cutting boards at most dollar stores.

1

Use markers to draw a picture on the smooth side of an acrylic cutting board.

2

Spray a thick sheet of paper with water. Use a paper towel to help spread the water around the paper. Press the wet side of the paper firmly against the cutting board, and rub for one minute. Carefully lift the paper from the board to reveal your print.

3

Create multiple prints and hang them on a wall to make your own art gallery!

TIP

If you use words in your artwork, remember to draw them backwards (looking in a mirror will help) so that they read the right way when you transfer the drawing!

silly faces

Markers are perfect for drawing funny faces! If you don't have a white marker, make sure you leave white circles for the eyes when you draw the faces.

Draw more silly faces! Practice on the opposite page.

PRACTICE HERE!

making stamps

Find something fun to stamp with! The flat rubber flower I used is a coaster. Try using leaves, bubble wrap, tree bark, buttons, pebbles, yarn, or string — the possibilities are endless!

MATERIALS

* Paper
* Stamp object
* Black ink pad
* Markers

1

Press your stamp object onto the ink pad and stamp the paper. It's okay if the object doesn't fit on the ink pad. You can stamp multiple times with different parts of the object, like I did.

2

When the ink is dry, start filling in the white parts of the design with markers. Use different colors and patterns.

Fill in all the white areas. Then add any extra details to complete your artwork. I added a stem to finish my flower!

colorful elephant

Turn your favorite animal into a fun and funky work of art! Follow along with this elephant. Then make your own patterned animals!

MATERIALS

* **Paper**
* **Pencil**
* **Ruler**
* **Markers**

1

Draw an elephant in pencil. Then trace the outline in black marker.

2

Use a ruler and black marker to create different sizes of triangles (or other shapes) inside the body.

3

Use markers to fill in each triangle with different colors and patterns. Then use a ruler and pencil to draw triangles in the background.

4

Trace the background triangles with a black marker. Then fill them in with color and patterns. What a crazy-looking elephant!

colored pencils

getting creative

Colored pencils work just like regular pencils, but they come in lots of colors. Below are some fun ways to use colored pencils. Try them on the opposite page!

COLORING DARK TO LIGHT

Press hard to create dark strokes. As you move down the paper, don't press as hard, making the color lighter as you go.

BLENDING COLORS

Color with one color from dark to light. Then use a second color to overlap the first. The two colors will blend together!

MIXING COLORS

Color over one color to make a new one. In this example, magenta on blue makes bright purple.

INDENTING

Press hard as you draw, indenting the paper. Then pick another color and lightly color over the drawing.

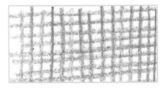

CRISSCROSS

Draw straight lines next to each other. Then turn the paper and draw more straight lines over the first set.

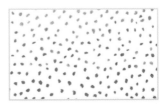

LOTS OF DOTS

Use lots of dots to color a drawing. The more dots in an area, the darker that area will look.

PRACTICE HERE

hot air balloons

Take your colored pencil skills to new heights by drawing this fleet of hot air balloons! Start by finding the hot air balloon drawing at the back of the book and gently tearing it out. Up, up, and away!

MATERIALS

* **Paper**
* **Pencil**
* **Colored pencils: sky blue, dark blue, light pink, dark pink, light green, dark green, orange, purple, and brown**

Color the background with a sky blue colored pencil. Color dark to light as you move down the paper so that the color is darker at the top and lighter at the bottom.

2

Color each stripe on the balloons dark to light. Make the top and bottom of each stripe darker than the center.

3

Use brown to color the balloon baskets and strings. Color dark to light again so that the centers of the baskets are lighter than the edges.

4

Color the top of the sky dark to light with a dark blue colored pencil. Then add light pink at the bottom of the sky.

5

Use dark pink and dark green colored pencils to outline the stripes on the balloons. Darken the tops and bottoms of the stripes with darker colors to make the balloons look more realistic!

rainbow doodles

Doodling a pattern is easy when you focus on one doodle at a time! Practice doodling your own pattern on page 57.

Draw a rainbow with your colored pencils.

2

Doodle more things, such as a big bow and a flower.

3

Keep going until you have seven or eight different doodles!

55

4

Repeat each doodle to create a pattern and fill the page. Try adding new doodles!

PRACTICE HERE

stained glass

Create your own stained-glass design with colored pencils and a black marker. You'll be surprised by the glowing results!

MATERIALS

* **Paper**   * **Black marker**   * **Colored pencils**

Find this drawing at the back of the book. Color in this design, and then try making your own!

Use a black marker to doodle lines and swirls on paper. Make sure the lines cross each other to create lots of shapes! Begin filling in the shapes with colored pencils. For a stained-glass look, color the edges a bit darker than the center of each shape.

2

◄ Color each shape dark to light so that the edges are darker than the centers.

3

► Use lots of colors to fill in all the shapes. Your masterpiece is complete!

watercolor paint

getting creative

It's easy to paint with watercolor! Just add water to the paint and watch the colors come alive! Below are some fun ways to paint with watercolor. Try them on a sheet of watercolor paper!

ADDING WATER

The more water you add to watercolor paint, the more the paper shows through, and the lighter the color will be.

SMOOTH PAINTING

Mix watercolor paint with a little bit of water. Use a paintbrush to stroke across the paper, overlapping the strokes to create an even color.

DARK TO LIGHT

Mix a little bit of water with watercolor paint, and start with dark strokes. Dip the brush in water as you add more strokes, making the paint lighter and lighter as you go.

TIP Clean your brushes with soap and warm water once you've finished painting.

BLENDING
Paint with one color at a time, rinsing your brush each time you pick a new color. The colors will blend smoothly together.

ROUGH PAINTING
Dip your paintbrush in paint, and dab it on a paper towel. Drag the brush lightly over the paper to create a rough texture.

USING SALT
Paint a section of paper and let the paint soak in. While the paint is wet, sprinkle a little salt on top. Once the paint is fully dry, wipe away the salt. This creates a spotty texture.

SPLATTERING
Dip your brush in paint, and run your finger over the bristles to create droplets of paint on the paper. Watch out—splattering can be very messy!

SPONGING
Dip a sponge in watered-down paint, and dab it lightly on your paper to create an interesting texture.

WET PAINTING
Brush plain water across the paper and let it soak in. While it is wet, pick a color and paint over the surface. Add a second color and watch the two colors blend together.

goldfish

Use wet painting to create this fancy goldfish scene. The colors blend together to look just like water!

MATERIALS

* Watercolor paper
* Pencil
* Watercolor paints: blue, blue-green, dark yellow, red-orange, brown, purple, and white

* Watercolor palette
* Large paintbrush
* Small paintbrush
* Jar of water

1

Use a pencil to draw a goldfish and sea plants on watercolor paper.

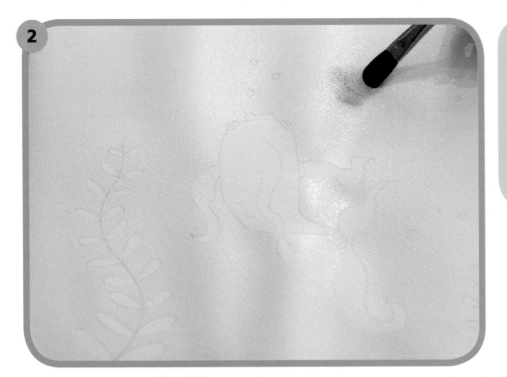

2

Use a large paintbrush to brush water on the paper around the fish and plants. Once you no longer see puddles of water on the paper, dip the brush in blue paint and begin to paint the water.

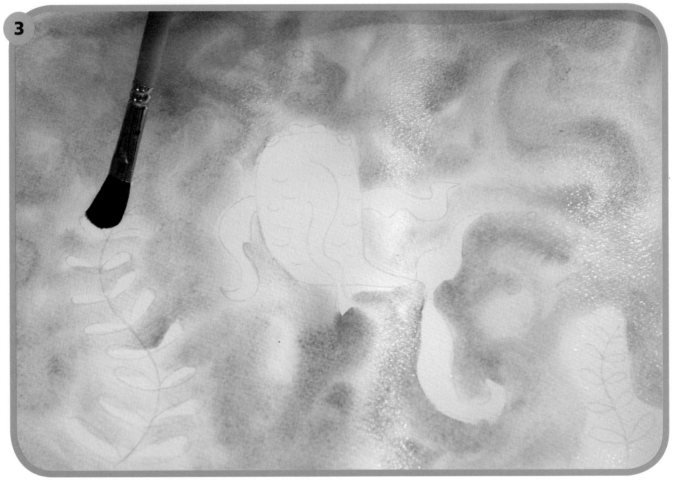

3

Fill the paper with blue swirls. Watch as the wet paper pulls the paint from the brush, making soft edges that look just like water! Continue adding blue paint throughout the water, stroking in swirls. Remember to avoid painting over the fish and plants.

4

Add blue-green paint in swirls around the blue. Let the paint dry.

Dip a small paintbrush in dark yellow watercolor paint, and paint the goldfish. Mix red and orange paint to add the fin details.

5

6

Use the red-orange mix to add more lines on the fins and tail. Then paint the lips. Use brown paint for the eyes.

7

Use purple to paint the sea plants.

8

Add bubbles with thick white watercolor paint. Your underwater scene is complete!

castle at sunset

This easy project shows you how to blend different colors into a pretty sunset. Then add the dark shadow of a fairy-tale castle!

MATERIALS

* Watercolor paper
* Masking or artist tape
* Pencil
* Watercolor paints: purple, magenta, orange, yellow, and black

* Watercolor palette
* Large paintbrush
* Small paintbrush
* Jar of water

1

Draw the outline of a castle on watercolor paper. Tape the edges of the paper to your painting surface to keep it in place. Put purple, magenta, orange, and yellow paint in your palette and add a little bit of water to each.

2

Use a large paintbrush to paint purple bands across the top of the sky.

3

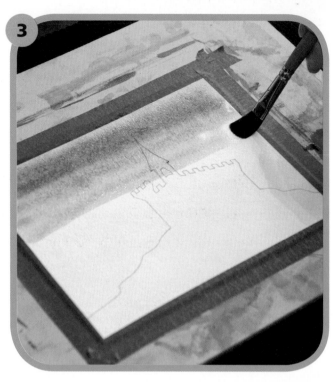

Rinse the brush. Dip it in the magenta paint and add more bands of color.

4

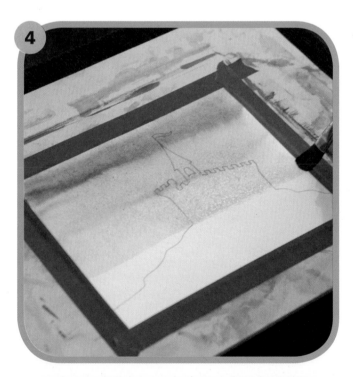

Rinse the brush and dip it in the orange paint. Add orange bands of color under the magenta.

5

Rinse the brush and finish the sky with yellow paint. Let the paint dry. Mix black and purple watercolor. Use a small paintbrush to paint the top of the castle.

6

Use a large paintbrush to finish painting the castle.

7

Use a small paintbrush to paint the flag and birds in the sky. Your masterpiece is complete!

acrylic paint

getting creative

Unlike watercolor paint, you can paint acrylic in thin or thick strokes. You can even paint light colors right over dark colors! This paint can be messy, so be sure to wear an apron while painting.

THICK OR THIN

You can paint with thick acrylic paint or thin it with water. When acrylic paint is thin, it feels like watercolor paint.

SMOOTH PAINTING

Mix a little bit of water with paint. Use a large paintbrush to evenly paint the paper.

BLENDING

Paint with one color first. Then dip your brush in a second color and overlap the strokes. Here, red and blue makes dark purple.

WIPING AWAY

You can wipe away thick acrylic paint to fix mistakes or create designs in the paint. Just wrap your finger in a tissue or paper towel and wipe the wet paint!

SCRAPING

Paint a thick layer of acrylic on your paper. Then use the end of a paintbrush handle to "draw," scraping into the paint.

ROUGH PAINTING

Dip your brush in paint, and dab it on a paper towel. Drag the brush lightly over the paper. This will create a rough texture.

SPONGING

Dip a sponge in watered-down paint, and dab it lightly on the paper. This will create an interesting texture.

SPLATTERING

Dip your brush in watered-down paint, and run your finger along the bristles to create droplets of paint on the paper. Watch out—splattering can be very messy!

DABBING

Dip the tip of your brush in paint, and dab it onto your paper. This texture is perfect for painting leaves on trees!

TIP

Keep your brushes wet in a jar of water while you're painting. Once you've finished, clean your brushes with soap and warm water.

wild painting

This project is colorful and messy — it's impossible to make a mistake! Create a wild acrylic painting with plastic wrap, marbles, and a cardboard box.

MATERIALS

* Canvas board or watercolor paper
* Acrylic paints
* Large paintbrush
* Plastic wrap
* Small cardboard box (such as a shoebox)
* Disposable cups or bowls
* Plastic spoon
* Marbles

1

Choose a background color, and thin the paint with water in a disposable bowl. Use a large paintbrush to cover a canvas board or sheet of watercolor paper.

2

Tear off a sheet of plastic wrap and press it over the painting, crinkling the plastic.

3

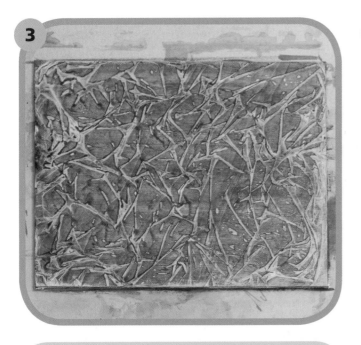

Peel off the wrap to see your new textured background!

4

Let the paint dry. Then put your painting in a cardboard box.

5

Pick a new color, and thin the paint with water in a new bowl. Add a few marbles to the bowl, and roll them around in the paint.

6

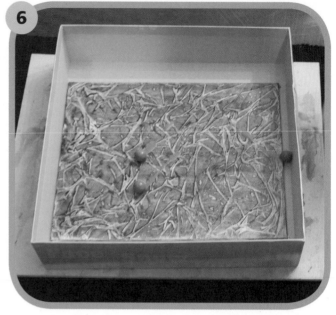

Use a plastic spoon to put the marbles on your painting. Tilt the box to roll the marbles around. When you're done, rinse off the marbles.

7

◄ Once the paint is dry, roll the marbles in a new color and place them in the box.

► You can add as many colors as you like! Add more texture by splattering paint across the art.

8

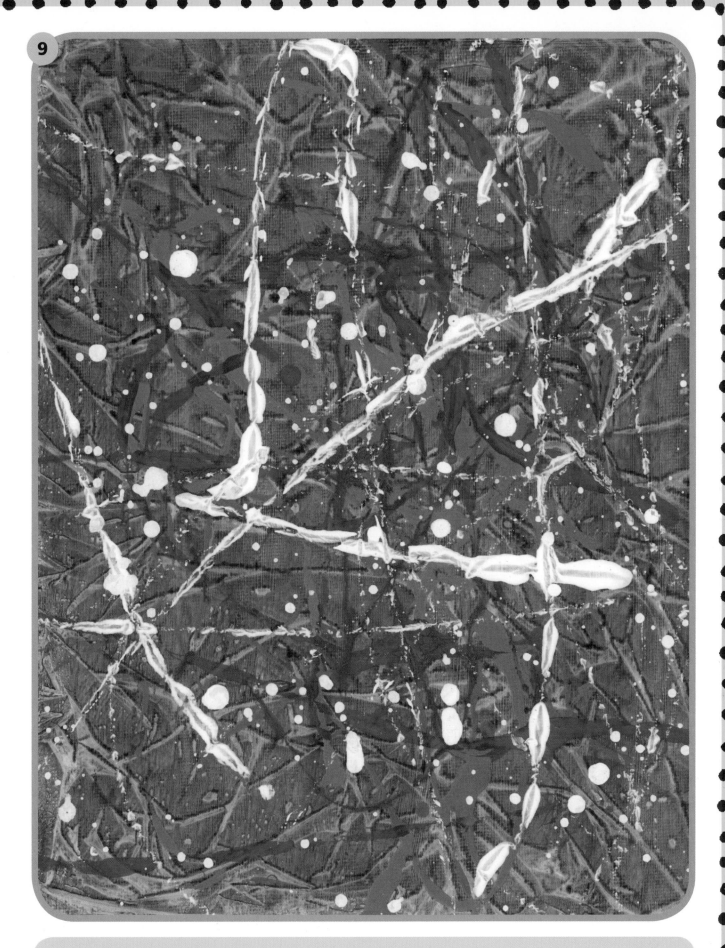

Let the painting dry completely before hanging your new masterpiece!

ice cream cone

A chocolate and strawberry ice cream cone? Yes, please!
Paint yourself a tasty treat with this easy acrylic project.
Use a sponge to make the ice cream look more realistic.
Yum!

MATERIALS

* Watercolor paper (or canvas board)
* Masking or artist tape
  (if using watercolor paper)
* Pencil
* Acrylic paints: white, green, brown,
  orange, and red
* Disposable bowls/plates
* Large paintbrush
* Medium paintbrush
* Small paintbrush
* Jar of water
* Sponge

1

Draw the ice cream cone on a sheet of watercolor paper (or canvas board). Tape the paper to your painting surface. Mix green and white paint in a bowl.

Paint the background with a large paintbrush. Don't paint the ice cream cone yet!

2

3

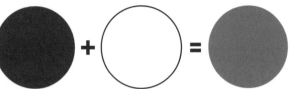

Create a chocolate paint color by mixing brown and white. Paint the bottom scoop.

4

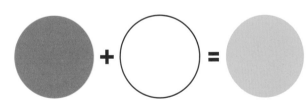

Mix a strawberry paint color by mixing red and white. Paint the top scoop.

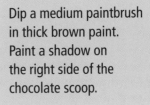

5

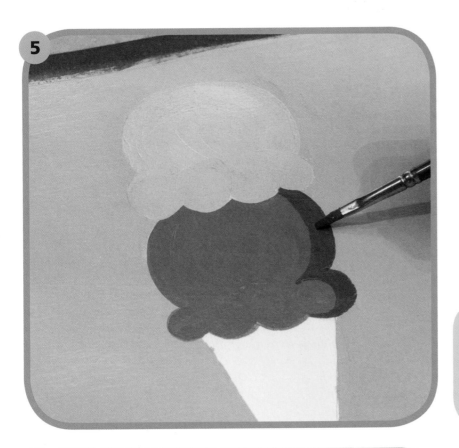

Dip a medium paintbrush in thick brown paint. Paint a shadow on the right side of the chocolate scoop.

6

Dip a sponge in the thick brown paint, and dab it on the shadow.

7

▲ Add a little more red paint to your strawberry mix, and paint a shadow on the right edge of the strawberry scoop.

8

Dip the sponge in the dark pink mix, and dab it on the right side of the scoop. Then dip the sponge in white paint, and dab the left side of both scoops.

9

◀ Now mix orange, white, and a little bit of brown. Paint the cone. Add more brown to the mix, and paint the shadow on the right side.

10

◀ Use a small paintbrush to add some crisscrossed brown lines on the cone.

11

▶ Let the paint to dry. Your ice cream cone looks good enough to eat!

WE ALL SCREAM FOR ICE CREAM!

garden critters

With acrylic paint, you can create both large and small paintings. In this project, use acrylic to paint little garden critters. Try combining them in a beautiful garden scene!

DRAGONFLY

1 Paint the dragonfly's body with blue-green paint.

2 Mix two light shades of purple. Use the darker mix to paint the top wings and the lighter mix to paint the bottom wings.

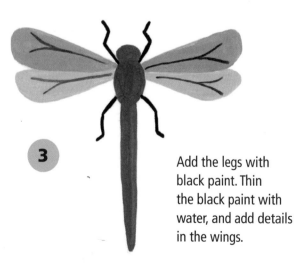

3 Add the legs with black paint. Thin the black paint with water, and add details in the wings.

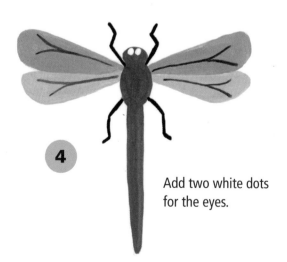

4 Add two white dots for the eyes.

SNAIL

Paint the snail's shell with brown paint.

Mix a little white into the brown paint. Dip your brush in the light brown mix, and dab it on a paper towel. Then rough paint along the edges of the shell.

Using bright green, paint the shape of the snail's body.

Add two white dots for the eyes. Once dry, dot on small black pupils and add the mouth.

LADYBUG

Paint a red oval or circle.

Using black paint, add the head and a line down the ladybug's back.

Add black dots on the red back.

Paint six black legs and the antennae. Then dot on two white eyes.

BEE

Paint a yellow oval.

Use black paint to add the head and bands along the body.

Add six legs, two antennae, and a small stinger. Let the paint dry.

Mix yellow and white paint with water. Add the wings, painting over the body and legs. Add two white dots for eyes.

BUTTERFLY

Paint the butterfly's body with black paint. Add two antennae.

Now outline the top half of each wing.

Outline the bottom half of each wing. Let the paint dry.

Use a bright color to paint the inside of each wing.

Use black paint to add details in the wings.

Add dots of white for the eyes and wing details.

CATERPILLAR

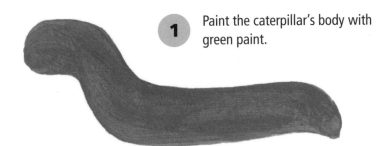

1 Paint the caterpillar's body with green paint.

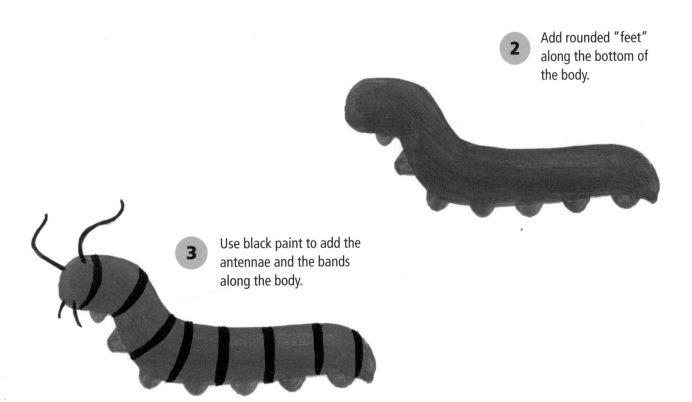

2 Add rounded "feet" along the bottom of the body.

3 Use black paint to add the antennae and the bands along the body.

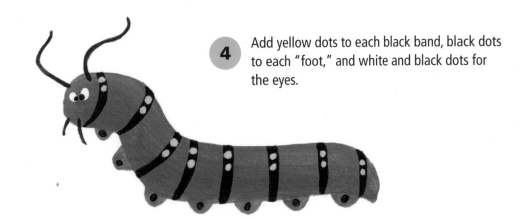

4 Add yellow dots to each black band, black dots to each "foot," and white and black dots for the eyes.

fill your palette

Use markers to fill in the paint palette.
Which colors would you choose?

chalk

getting creative

It's fun to make art with chalk! Try out these fun ways to use chalk on thick drawing paper!

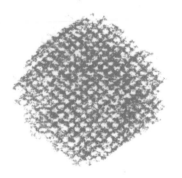

COLORING

Hold your chalk like a crayon, and color across the paper.

SMUDGING

Color with chalk on the paper. Then rub it gently with a tissue, paper towel, or blending stump.

LAYERING

Build a chalk drawing in layers. Try smudging your first layer. Then draw with a new color on top.

BLENDING

Blend two colors together by smudging between them with a tissue or blending stump.

Chalk is very easy to smudge, so be sure to keep your hands off the paper as you draw.

CHOOSING A PAPER TEXTURE

Different types of paper will make your chalk drawing look different. Which texture do you prefer?

Smooth Paper

Textured Paper

Laid Paper

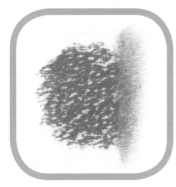

Watercolor Paper

COLORED PAPER

Colored paper can help make your drawings more realistic. See how easy it is to draw a round ball using just black and white chalk on gray paper?

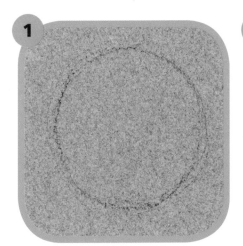

1

Use black to lightly draw a circle.

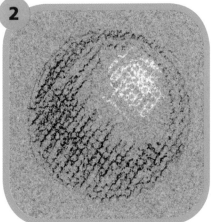

2

Color a "C" shape for the shadow. Add a white highlight on the top right side.

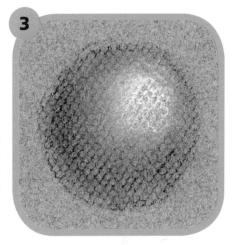

3

Blend the chalk in a circular motion.

Try dipping chalk into water before drawing on thick paper. The color will be extra smooth and creamy!

chalk doodles

Warm up by doodling on a chalkboard! Practice drawing all kinds of lines, shapes, and doodles.

With a chalkboard, cleanup is easy! Simply wipe it clean with an eraser or paper towel when you're ready to draw something else.

roses in bloom

Use chalk on colored paper to really make your artwork stand out! In this project, the orange paper makes the purple vase "pop" off the page!

MATERIALS

* Orange paper
* Pencil
* Chalk
* Tissue

1

Draw a vase and flowers with your pencil. Then use dark purple chalk to color the edges of the vase.

2

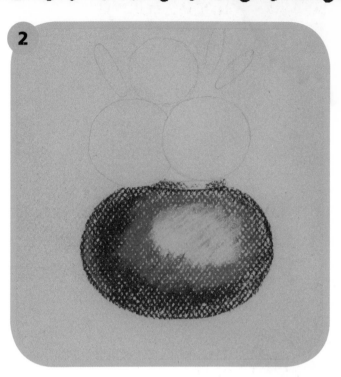

Use two lighter shades of purple to fill in the center of the vase.

3

Blend the three colors together with a tissue. Then add a white highlight on the vase.

4

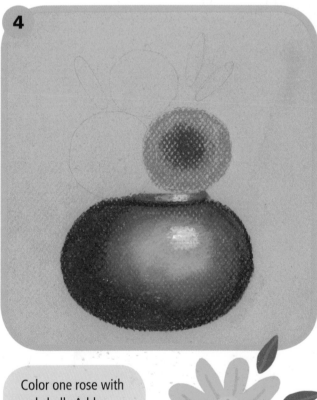

Color one rose with red chalk. Add a darker brown circle in the center.

5

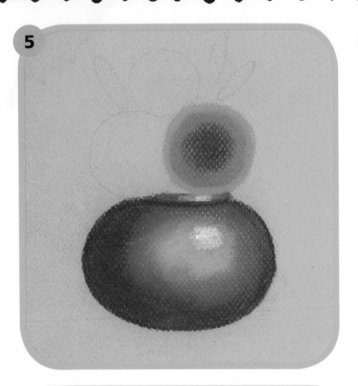

Outline the red circle with pink, and blend the colors together with a tissue.

6

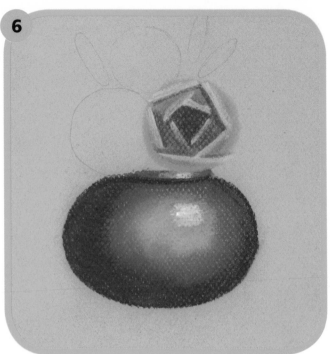

Use light pink chalk to add lines for the petals.

7

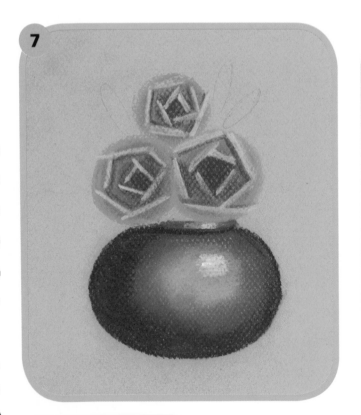

Make two more roses.

8

Add purple flowers around the roses. Add light purple and white chalk on the right side of the purple flowers to make them look more realistic.

9

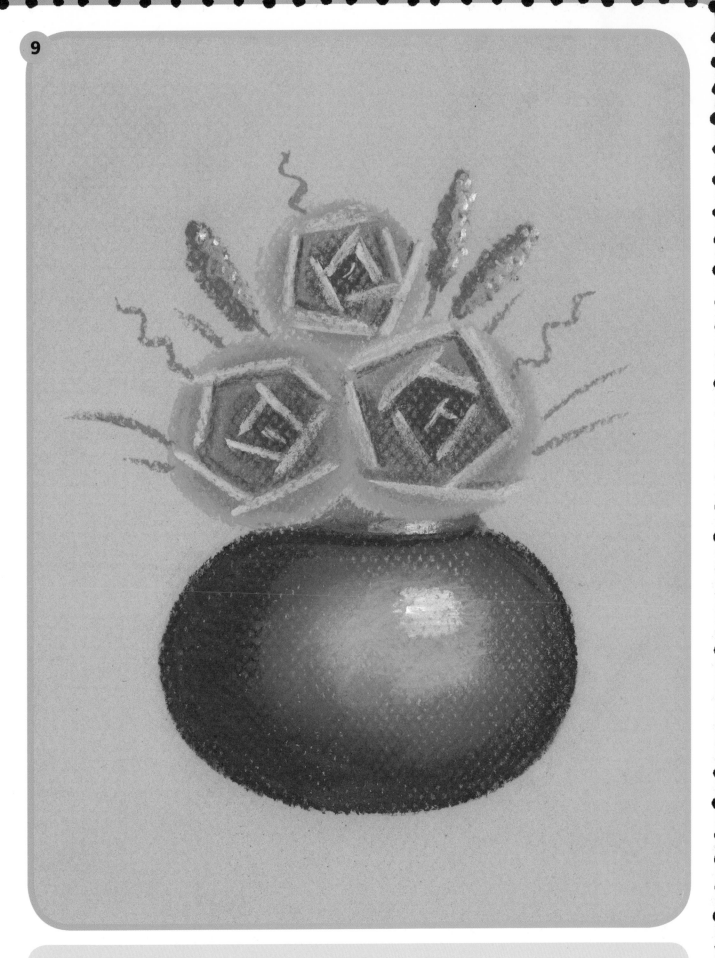

Draw green lines and squiggles for the leaves, and you're done!

CHALK

bird nest

In this project, use soft blends and rough strokes to make a cute bird nest. Use a blending stump to blend small details in your drawing.

MATERIALS

* Textured drawing paper
* Pencil
* Eraser
* Chalk: reddish brown, dark brown, light brown, dark blue, light blue, white, pink, orange, black, and turquoise
* Blending stump
* Sandpaper
* Tissue or paper towels

1

Draw the birds and nest on a sheet of textured drawing paper.

2

Fill in the nest with reddish-brown chalk, coloring around the eggs. Then smooth the color with a blending stump.

3

Use dark brown chalk to darken the middle of the nest. Then draw twigs on the outside of the nest.

4

Use light brown chalk to draw more twigs on the nest.

5

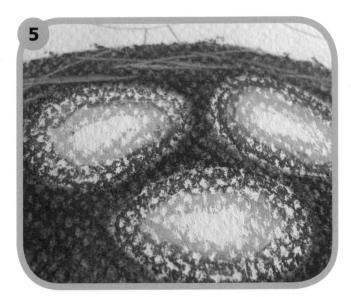

Use dark blue chalk to color the outside edges of the eggs. Add light blue chalk inside the dark blue. Leave a little white in the middle of each egg.

6

Smooth the chalk with the blending stump. Smudge the color into the middle of the eggs.

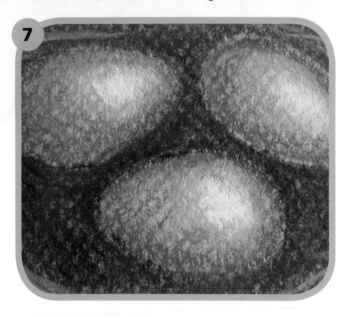

7

Add white highlights on the eggs.

8

Color one bird with pink chalk, and blend the color. Add the legs and beak with orange chalk. Dot the eye with black chalk. Use a little bit of white chalk for the bird's wing.

9

Color the second bird with turquoise chalk. Add the beak, legs, eye, and wing. Your bird nest is now complete!

getting creative

With mixed media art, you can use any art tools.
There are no rules! Here are some tips
for getting started.

SURFACES

Try making mixed media art on paper,
wood, cardboard, fabric, and canvas.

GLUE

Use glue to add papers, ribbons, and other
things to mixed media art.

PAPERS

You can use all kinds of papers in your projects. Scrapbook paper, wrapping paper, magazines, and other thick papers work well.

STAMPS & STENCILS

Use stamps and stencils to create cool textures and backgrounds in your artwork. You can stamp with almost anything. Try using jar lids, sponges, bubble wrap, felt coasters, and even fruits and veggies!

PAINT

You can use both acrylic and watercolor paint in mixed media art. Try combining paint with other tools and see what happens!

CRAYONS

Use crayons to color your artwork. Try painting watercolor paint over crayon for a cool effect!

tree blowing

Use a straw to blow paint across the paper to make the leaves of this tree. Use any colors you like — electric blue, bright green, even purple!

MATERIALS

* Watercolor paper
* Watercolor paints
* Straw

* Dictionary pages
* Scissors
* Glue stick

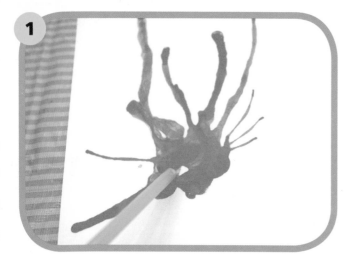

▲ Make a small watery puddle of paint on the top half of the paper. Blow gently through a straw to spread the paint.

▶ Try again with another color. Soon you will have a tree full of leaves!

3

◄ Let the paint dry.
Cut a tree trunk shape
out of dictionary pages
or other paper and
glue it on the bottom
half of the paper.

4

► Cut tree branches
out of the paper and
glue them in place.
Your tree is finished!

funny face

Use cookie cutters to make a funny face
on a colorful background.

MATERIALS

* Watercolor paper
* Watercolor paints
* Paintbrushes
* Pencil
* Cookie cutters
* Black marker

Add colorful
splotches of
watercolor paint
on the paper.
The more color,
the better!

2

◀ Let each color dry before you add a new one. This keeps the colors bright.

3

▶ Time to add the face! Make eyes, a nose, and a mouth with cookie cutters.

4

Trace the cookie cutter shapes with a pencil.

5

Trace the outlines with a black marker. Then finish your funny face with hair and ears.

3-D flowers

Create pretty flowers all year long with this easy project!
You can make the flowers any shape you wish.

MATERIALS

* Cardboard
* Chipboard
* Scrapbook paper
* Paintbrush

* Acrylic paints
* Glue stick
* Glue dots
* Scissors

* Hole punch
* Markers
* Twine

1

Paint the cardboard first. Try using two colors! Paint one color, and let it dry. Then paint a second color on top. Let the bottom color peek through.

▶ Cut three shapes out of chipboard for each flower—one large, one medium, and one small!

2

3

◀ Glue a piece of scrapbook paper onto each shape. Make each flower by attaching the large, medium, and small shapes to each other with glue dots. Cut out a paper vase, and glue it to the cardboard. Then add the flowers with glue dots.

4

Use markers to outline the vase and add dots or other decorations to the flowers. Don't forget to add stems!

5

Punch two holes at the top of the cardboard, and use twine to hang your new masterpiece!

waxy watercolor

Combining crayons with watercolor paint is a fun way to bring art to life! Crayons are made of wax, which repels water. That means you can paint over your drawing and it will show through!

MATERIALS

* Watercolor paper
* Crayons
* Watercolor paints

* Paintbrush
* Construction paper (optional)
* Scissors (optional)

1

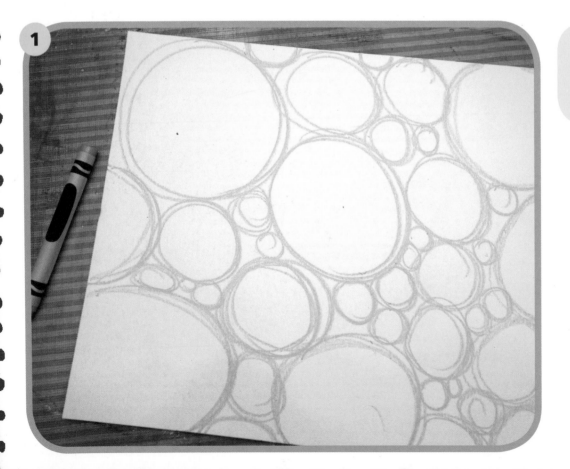

Draw a pattern with a crayon all over the paper, from edge to edge.

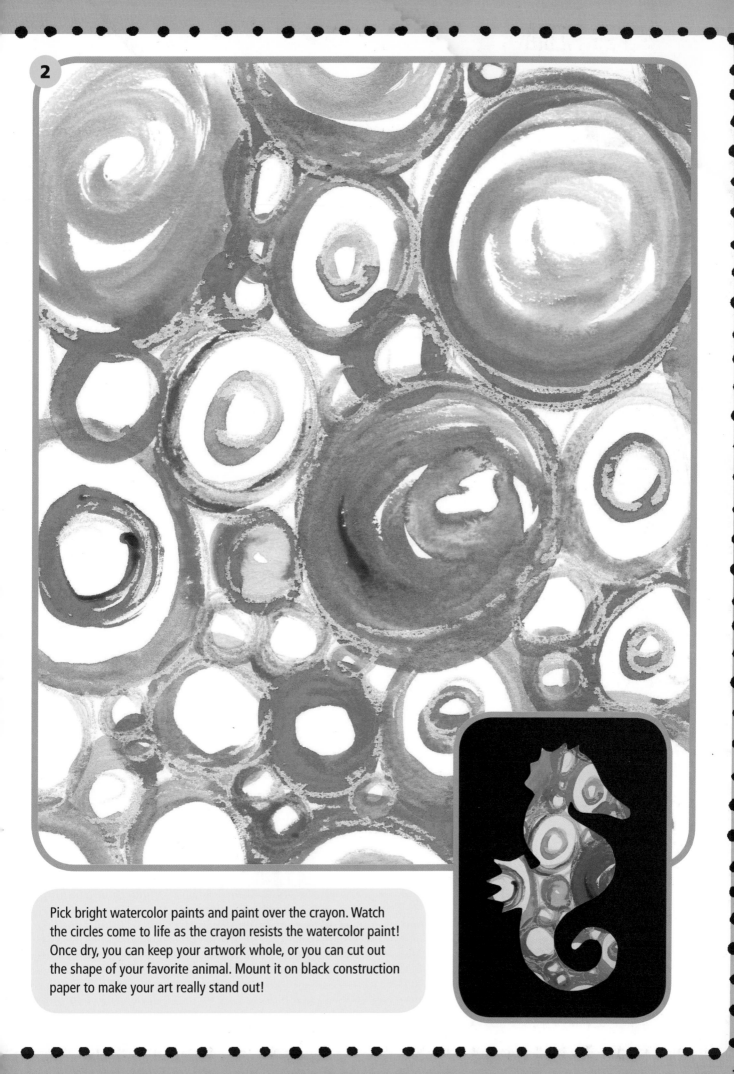

2

Pick bright watercolor paints and paint over the crayon. Watch the circles come to life as the crayon resists the watercolor paint! Once dry, you can keep your artwork whole, or you can cut out the shape of your favorite animal. Mount it on black construction paper to make your art really stand out!

snowman

Create this winter wonderland, using crayons and watercolor paints!

MATERIALS

* Watercolor paper
* Masking or artist tape
* Pencil
* Watercolor paints: blue and purple
* Watercolor palette
* Large paintbrush
* Small paintbrush
* Jar of water
* Crayons

1

Tape the watercolor paper to your work surface. Then draw a snowman.

2

Use crayon to color the snowman's orange carrot nose and green scarf. Crisscross lines on the hat to create a woolly texture.

3

Use a dark green crayon to color the trees in the distance.

4

Add black dots for the eyes, mouth, and buttons. Draw the brown arms. Color the snowman's body white, and add dots in the sky for falling snow.

5

Paint the top of the sky with dark blue watercolor paint. You can paint right over the white dots!

6

Add water to the dark blue paint and paint the rest of the sky dark to light.

7

Use a tissue or paper towel to wipe up extra paint from the crayon, especially over the snowman.

8

Paint the snowy ground light purple.

LET IT SNOW!

9

Use darker purple to add the snowman's shadow. Your winter wonderland is complete!

the end

Now that you know how to work with crayons, markers, colored pencils, paint, and chalk, the sky is the limit! Create every day, and watch the artist inside of you blossom and grow. Every piece of artwork is unique—just like you!